E U C H A R I S T

Sacred Meal, Sacrifice, Real Presence

STUDY GUIDE

A Catholic Study Program presented by
BISHOP ROBERT BARRON

Study Guide written by
BISHOP ROBERT BARRON,
ROBERT MIXA & ROZANN LEE

✛ *THIRD EDITION* ✛

Word on FIRE

www.WORDONFIRE.org
© 2018 Word on Fire Catholic Ministries

EUCHARIST
Sacred Meal, Sacrifice, Real Presence

TABLE OF CONTENTS

Bishop Robert Barron
Robert Mixa
Rozann Lee

A DEEPER LOOK *at the* EUCHARIST

Welcome to Bishop Robert Barron's in-depth study on the Eucharist, the "source and summit of the Christian life."[CCC 1324]

This guide is designed to help you apply to your life what you will learn from Bishop Barron's look at the Catholic Tradition. The aim is to help you study, reflect upon, and act in obedience to the will of God in Christ. You will have the chance to dig into the Catholic Tradition and grapple with Scripture and the Church's teaching as it is summarized in the *Catechism of the Catholic Church*. You will also be able to use the materials provided in Bishop Barron's presentation in order to assess and enhance your life as a disciple of Jesus Christ. The core of each guide is the QUESTIONS FOR UNDERSTANDING and the QUESTIONS FOR APPLICATION, which will reinforce the main points made in each section of Bishop Barron's presentation on the different aspects of the Eucharist.

Throughout the study, you will be asked to reference different Bible verses and passages. We recommend the *New American Bible* or the *Revised Standard Version*, or you can also use another acceptable Catholic translation. To answer the questions, you will need to refer to the *Catechism of the Catholic Church*, which can be purchased at your local bookstore or found online at: *www.scborromeo.org/ccc.htm*.

Over the course of this study, we will examine three important aspects of this inexhaustibly rich Sacrament: the Eucharist as sacred meal, as sacrifice, and as real presence. These elements unite the Church across time and unite us to our fellow Catholics in every sacred liturgy.

Before we begin looking at these three aspects in detail, let's consider the importance of the Eucharist in our Faith. The Eucharist is not a luxury, but a necessity, for without it, in the spiritual sense, we would starve to death. The fathers of the second Vatican Council expressed this truth in an oft-repeated phrase from the document *Lumen Gentium* that the Eucharist is the source and summit of the Christian life. It is both the fountain from which life in Christ flows and the goal toward which it tends; it is the alpha and the omega of Christian discipleship; it is the energy without which authentic Christianity runs down.

Without the Eucharist, we could be a pious congregation of like-minded people or a society dedicated to the memory and teaching of Jesus, but we couldn't possibly be the Church. As Saint John Paul II argued in what was, fittingly enough, his last encyclical, *Ecclesia de Eucharistia* (the Church comes from the Eucharist), the Body and Blood of Jesus are not simply the sacred objects at the center of the Church's concern; they *are* the church, its lifeblood and raison d'etre.

In one of his sermons on the Eucharist, the great English Catholic preacher Ronald Knox made the following observation. The vast majority of Jesus' commands — to love one's enemies, to turn the other cheek, to forgive seventy times seven times, etc. — have been rather consistently disregarded. However, Knox says there is one command of Jesus that has, up and down the centuries, been massively obeyed. Throughout the long history of the Church, through a whole series of dramatic successes and failures, despite the stupidity and wickedness of so many Christians, the command "do this in memory of me" has been and continues to be obeyed. It is as though Christians, in all of their sin, have realized from the beginning that the spiritual life depends upon the Eucharist the way that physical life depends upon food, oxygen, and water. And so, despite themselves, they do what Jesus told them to do in his memory.

The topic of the Eucharist is huge and multivalent. Thousands of treatises, essays, sermons, and reflections have been dedicated to it over the centuries. Its mysteries and dimensions are endless precisely because the Eucharist is Christ, the one in whom, according to St. Paul, are hidden all the treasures of wisdom and knowledge (Col. 2:3). One could easily construct an entire systematic theology around the central motif of the Eucharist, showing how it is intimately related to the doctrines of creation, revelation, Christology, grace, redemption, and the last things. However, Bishop Barron follows the lead of many Eucharistic commentators and focuses on three major themes: meal, sacrifice, and Real Presence.

The Eucharist is, first, the great meal of fellowship that God wants to establish with his people, the joyful bond in which the divine life is shared spiritually and physically with a hungry world. There are many examples of the sacred meal throughout Scripture. However, communion in a fallen world is impossible without sacrifice. In a universe that has become twisted and off-kilter, beset by division, hatred, and fear, the establishment of real love and justice will come only

© 2018 Word on Fire Catholic Ministries

at the price of suffering. Hence, the Eucharist is also the embodiment of Jesus' great act of sacrificial suffering on the cross at Calvary. At the Last Supper, Jesus said "take this all of you and drink from it; this is the cup of my Blood." What the disciples are invited to consume is the very self that Jesus offers in sacrifice. What we eat and drink at the fellowship meal, therefore, is nothing other than the death of Jesus, the act by which he gave himself away for the salvation of the world.

Both themes of sacred meal and sacrifice are gathered up and given full expression in the Catholic doctrine of the "real" presence of Jesus in the Eucharist. Though it contains a symbolic dimension, the Eucharist is more than a symbol, more than a concoction, however moving and evocative, of our own religious imagination. In it, Jesus is present to us through his own power and in his dense objectivity as both food and sacrificial offering. There is something terrible and uncontrollable in the *reality* of the presence. The Eucharist is not our product, but our Lord, and as such, it calls us to conversion.

In this interweaving of meal, sacrifice, and Real Presence, we discover the heart of a Catholic Eucharistic theology.

QUESTIONS FOR UNDERSTANDING

1. Read *Catechism of the Catholic Church* (CCC) 1324-1327. What does it mean to say that the Eucharist is the "source and summit of the Christian life"? What do we mean by "source," and what do we mean by "summit"?

2. Read CCC 1328, 1359-1361. What is the meaning of the word "eucharist"?

© 2018 Word on Fire Catholic Ministries

3. Now, read Philippians 2:5-8 and CCC 1362-64. In receiving the Eucharist and understanding the meaning of the word, for what are we "grateful"? How does the reception of the Eucharist in the Holy Sacrifice of the Mass express this gratitude?

4. Read CCC 1329-1332 about the other common names for the Eucharist. List some of those names and their meanings.

5. Read I Corinthians 10:16-17 and Romans 12:4-5. How does the way we participate in the Body and Blood of Christ during the Mass define who we are as we exit church?

6. Read Luke 22:17-20 and CCC 1342 and 1345. Bishop Barron, in his book *Eucharist*, says that "Throughout the long history of the church, throughout the whole series of dramatic successes and failures, despite the stupidity and wickedness of so many Christians, the command, 'Do this in memory of me' has been and continues to be obeyed."[1] What does this say about the role of the Eucharist in the life of the Church throughout history? In other words, how are we a "Eucharistic people"?

[1] Barron, Robert. *Eucharist* (2007, Orbis Books, NY), pg. 10.

   © 2018 *Word on Fire Catholic Ministries*

QUESTIONS FOR APPLICATION

1. Bishop Barron tells of his experience as a Eucharistic minister at St. Peter's Basilica in Rome, saying that he had the distinct feeling that he was distributing the Eucharist to people who were "starving for it." Have you, during a prescribed fast or otherwise, ever felt as if you were "starving"? How did it feel when you were finally able to eat? Have you ever been starving for the Eucharist? What was it like when you were able to partake in the Sacrament? What are the similarities and differences in those two experiences?

2. Read the description of the meal presented in the movie *Babette's Feast* in the excerpt from Bishop Barron's *Eucharist* book that is provided in the online support materials (https://www.wordonfire.org/wof-site/media/eucharistbabettesfeastpdf.pdf). How does a feast like this serve as a metaphor of the Eucharist? Have you ever hosted or participated in a feast like the one described? As the host, what was your motivation for having the feast? As a guest, what was memorable about the experience, and how did you feel toward the host?

3. How is Babette Christ-like? In what distinct ways does she empty herself in love for her guests? In what concrete ways can you participate in even greater generosity and humility in seemingly ordinary situations?

© 2018 Word on Fire Catholic Ministries

SACRED MEAL

The *Sacrum Convivium*, or Sacred Banquet, is continually presented and represented throughout the Old and New Testaments. Bishop Barron depicts multiple occurrences of this sacred banquet: the story of Adam and Eve in the Garden of Eden; the sacred banquet on God's holy mountain of Zion with his people, Israel; the miraculous feast of loaves and fishes that Jesus provides for his followers; and the "Last Supper" that Jesus shares with his Apostles.

Sacred Meal in the Old Testament

Genesis tells us that God placed Adam and Even in the midst of a garden of earthly delights and gave them permission to eat from all of the trees in the garden except one (Gen. 2:15-17). He instructed them, in short, to participate in his life through the joy of eating and drinking. But what about the prohibition? Why is the tree of the knowledge of good and evil forbidden to them? The fundamental determination of good and evil remains, necessarily, the prerogative of God alone, since God is, himself, the ultimate good. To seize this knowledge, therefore, is to claim divinity for oneself — and this is the one thing that a creature can never really do and thus should never try. If we turn ourselves into God, then the link that ought to connect us, through God, to the rest of creation is lost, and we find ourselves alone and not able to participate in the sacred banquet of communion with God or with others through God.

This is the nature of sin across the ages. God wants us to eat and drink in communion with him and our fellow creatures, but our own fear and pride break up the party. God wants us gathered around him in gratitude and love, but our resistance results in scattering, isolation, and violence. God wants the sacred meal; we want to eat alone and on our terms. But the God of the Bible is relentless in his love. He will not rest until this situation is rectified. The whole of the scriptural story can be seen as a coherent narrative of God's attempt to restore the fallen creation, to reestablish the joy of the banquet.

Two additional Old Testament presentations of the sacred meal are the Passover meal and the feast on the Lord's mountain as described by the prophet Isaiah. The Passover meal was established by God on the night he set the Israelites free from slavery in Egypt and was to be repeated as a ritual meal for all succeeding generations as a "perpetual institution" (Ex. 12:14).

As God led the Israelites out of slavery, which is to say, bondage to sin, God established a meal that united the whole people around a common table and a common food. And he declared that this act of unity must be repeated down through the ages as the defining gesture of the Israelite nation. The Passover meal was a recovery (however imperfect) of the easy unity and fellowship in the Garden of Eden; God hosting a banquet at which his human creatures share life with him and each other.

The second instance of Old Testament meal symbolism that Bishop Barron explores is found in the book of the prophet Isaiah. One of Isaiah's master images, on display throughout his writings, is the holy mountain. Isaiah dreams of the coming together of all the scattered tribes of Israel, indeed of the whole world, around the worship of the one, true God. All nations will stream toward the "mountain of the Lord's house," which is Zion, where the temple or the place of right worship is situated. Having found friendship with God, human beings will rediscover friendship with one another, creating total, cosmic peace. Along with right worship and peace, Isaiah adds a third feature of God's holy mountain — a magnificent meal. In his vision, the gathered community is fed by a gracious God with the finest foods, calling to mind the situation in the Garden of Eden before the eating and drinking was interrupted by a grasp at godliness.

Sacred Meal in the New Testament

Since one of the principal desires of Yahweh was to reestablish the sacred meal, it should be no surprise that Jesus would make the sacred meal central to his messianic work. Throughout his public ministry, Jesus gathered people around a table of fellowship. In his time, the table was a place where the divisions and stratifications of society were particularly on display, but at Jesus' table, all were welcome: saints and sinners, the just and the unjust, the healthy and the sick, men and women. This open table fellowship was not simply a challenge to the societal status quo, but also an expression of God's deepest intentions vis-a-vis the human

© 2018 Word on Fire Catholic Ministries

race. In fact, very often Jesus' most profound teaching took place at table, calling to mind Isaiah's holy mountain where a festive meal would be spread out and where "instruction" would go forth.

This fellowship started as early as Jesus' birth when he was wrapped in swaddling clothes and "laid in a manger," the place where the animals eat. Jesus had come to be food for a hungry world. He was destined to be, not only the host at the sacred banquet, but the meal itself. And to Christ's manger came the shepherds (evocative of the poor and marginalized) and kings (evocative of the nations of the world), drawn there as though by a magnet. Thus commenced the realization of Isaiah's vision.

A story that can be found in all three of the synoptic Gospels is that of the conversion of Levi (or Matthew) the tax collector. We hear that as Jesus was passing by, he spotted Matthew at his tax collector's post. Jesus gazed at this man and said, simply, "Follow me." Matthew, we are told, immediately got up and followed the Lord. But where did he follow him? To a banquet! "While he was at table in his house ..." is the first thing we read after the declaration that Matthew followed him. Before he calls Matthew to do anything, before he sends him on mission, Jesus invites Matthew to recline in easy fellowship around a festive table. Erasmo Leiva-Merikakis comments, "The deepest meaning of Christian discipleship is not to work for Jesus but to be with Jesus." The former tax collector listens to the Word, laughs with him, breaks bread with him, and in this finds his true identity.

The miracle of the feeding of the thousands with a few loaves and fishes can be found in all four Gospels. These narratives are richly iconic presentations of the great theme of the sacred meal. In Luke's account (Luke 9:10-17), crowds gather to hear Jesus teach and to bring their sick to him for cures. It gets late and the disciples want to dismiss the crowds so they can get something to eat, but Jesus tells them to "give them some food yourselves." But they protest: "Five loaves and two fish are all we have." Jesus instructs the disciples to gather the crowd. Then, taking the loaves and fishes, Jesus says a blessing over them, breaks them, and gives them to the disciples for distribution. Everyone ate until they were satisfied.

The hungry people who gather around Jesus are symbolic of the hungry human race, starving from the time of Adam and Eve for what will satisfy. In imitation of our first parents, we have tried to satisfy our hunger with wealth, pleasure, power, and honor, but none of it works, precisely because we have all been wired for God and God is nothing but love. It is only when we conform ourselves to the way of love, only when, in a high paradox, we contrive to empty out the ego, that we are filled. Thus the five loaves and two fish symbolize that which has been given to us, all that we have received as a grace, from God. If we hang onto it, we lose it. But if we turn it over to Christ, then we will find it transfigured and multiplied, even unto the feeding of the world.

Bishop Barron calls this the "loop of grace." God offers, as a sheer grace, the gift of being, but if we try to cling to that gift and make it our own (in the manner of Adam and Eve), we lose it. The constant command of the Bible is this: what you have received as a gift, give as a gift — and you will find the original gift multiplied and enhanced. God's grace, precisely because it is grace, cannot be held on to; rather, it is had only in the measure that it remains grace, that is to say, a gift given away.

All of these themes are summed up and drawn together in the meal that Jesus hosted the night before his death. Luke tells us that, at the climactic moment of his life and ministry, Jesus "took his place at table with the apostles" (Luke 22:14-20). At this Last Supper, Jesus, in a culminating way, embodied Yahweh's desire to sit in easy intimacy with his people, sharing his life with them. He said, "I have eagerly desired to eat this Passover with you before I suffer."

What stood at the heart of this event? Jesus took the unleavened bread of the Passover, the bread symbolic of Israel's hasty flight from slavery to freedom, blessed it in accord with the traditional Passover prayer of blessing, broke it and distributed it to his disciples saying, "This is my body, which will be given for you; do this in memory of me." And then after they had eaten, he took a cup of wine and said, "This cup is the new covenant in my blood, which will be shed for you." Acting once more in the very person of Yahweh, Jesus fed his friends with his very substance. To say "body" and "blood" in the context of first-century Judaism, is to say "self," and thus Jesus was inviting his disciples to feed on him and thereby to draw his life into theirs, conforming themselves to him in the most intimate and complete way possible. We must never keep the account of the fall far from our minds when we consider these events. If our trouble began with a bad meal (seizing at godliness on our own terms), then our salvation commences with a rightly structured meal (God offering us his life as a free gift). What was foreshadowed when Mary laid the Christ child in the manger came, at this meal, to full expression.

This entire story — creation, the fall, the formation of Israel, the Passover to freedom, the vision of Isaiah's holy mountain, the gracious table fellowship of Jesus, the Last Supper, the heavenly banquet — is made present to us at the Mass. The Eucharistic liturgy of the Church sums up and re-expresses the history of salvation, culminating in the meal by which Jesus feeds us with his very self.

   © 2018 Word on Fire Catholic Ministries

These biblical feasts demonstrate what God intends for each one of us: to unite us in peaceful, life-giving, holy, and eternal communion with himself and with one another as a faithful people. He intends to share an eternal meal with us — a meal that will draw us deeper into himself and will satisfy our ultimate hunger. On this side of heaven, the fullest way we can participate in this meal is to partake of the sacred, Eucharistic banquet.

QUESTIONS FOR UNDERSTANDING

1. Read CCC 1391-1397. What specific graces does Holy Communion confer on those who receive it?

2. Read Isaiah 2:1-5, depicting God's holy mountain. What happens on God's holy mountain that also happens in the Mass?

3. Read Matthew 9:9-13 (the conversion of Matthew) and CCC 1348. What is the first thing Jesus does before Matthew commences his vocation as Jesus' disciple? What does Bishop Barron suggest as the reason?

4. Read Matthew 14:13-21. This miracle is a wonderful depiction of the "Loop of Grace," which is presented by Bishop Barron as the beautiful way in which our ultimate, thankful sacrifice leads to God's overflowing grace. How is this exemplified in the Mass? How does Bishop Barron say Adam and Eve interrupted the "Loop of Grace"? How does sin perpetuate these interruptions?

 © 2018 Word on Fire Catholic Ministries

5. What, according to Bishop Barron, is the significance of the baby Jesus being placed in the manger? How does this relate to the Last Supper and to the Eucharist that we receive during the Holy Sacrifice of the Mass?

QUESTIONS FOR APPLICATION

1. Bishop Barron quotes the theologian Pseudo-Dionysius the Areopagite in saying that God creates the world because he is Goodness Itself, and "the Good is diffusive of itself," [1] meaning it cannot help but overflow. In God's case, it overflows into the creative energy from which the world emerges. Have you ever known someone that you would consider truly "good"? In what way did he/she "overflow" that prompted you to recognize that goodness? Did he/she draw you to participate in this goodness? How?

[1] Barron, Robert. *Eucharist* (2007, Orbis Books, NY), pg. 28.

2. Have you ever considered the idea that Bishop Barron presents: "...the world, in its entirety, has been loved into existence"? How can knowing that you are continually being loved into existence affect your attitude and behavior each day, both in the way you treat yourself and in the way you treat others?

3. Bishop Barron points out that God establishes a people Israel as a magnet for the world, an example of right worship united by the Passover meal — their own *Sacrum Convivium*. We, too, are called to be "magnets" for the world, offering our lives as the primary testimony to the truth of the Faith. In what way have we, like the people Israel, ventured away from right worship? What are some specific areas of our lives that we can improve in order to draw more people into the Sacred Banquet?

© 2018 Word on Fire Catholic Ministries

4. In the story of the multiplication of the loaves and fishes, why do the disciples want to dismiss the people? How does this reflect our own tendency to "take matters into our own hands"? What is the root of this behavior?

NOTES:

© 2018 Word on Fire Catholic Ministries

SACRIFICE

Bishop Barron reminds us: "In a world gone wrong, there is no communion without sacrifice." Sacrifice is essential to understanding salvation history as a divine rescue mission that returns humanity to the fellowship Adam and Eve had with God prior to the Fall. God sets himself the task of saving his compromised creation, and the principal means that he chooses is the formation of a people who would learn to walk in his ways and would become thereby a light to all the nations.

The first step in building up the people, Israel, is the call of Abram of Ur who would become Abraham, the father of Israel. "Now the Lord said to Abram, 'Go from your country and your kindred and your father's house to the land that I will show you. I will make of you a great nation …'" (Gen. 12:1-2). The essential problem began with disobedience, and thus the solution must begin with obedience. Eve and Adam became rebels; Abram must, accordingly, become a servant. He is being told to uproot his entire life and to move, to a distant land he knows nothing about — and he is, we are informed, 75 years old.

To cling to godliness, in the manner of our first parents, is to claim lordship over one's own life; to surrender to God is to realize that one's life is not one's own, that a higher and more compelling voice commands. In all of this, we sense that friendship with God (a covenant with him) would involve sacrifice, the abandonment of the self. If Abram can contrive a way to make of his life a gift — if he can sacrifice in trust what God has given to him — then his being will increase: "I will make of you a great nation."

So Abram, in faith, sets out with his family. The rest of the biblical narrative, up to and including the story of Jesus, is the account of God's formation of the clan of Abram, a people after his own heart, through intertwined themes of covenant and sacrifice. Abram is obedient, so God makes a covenant with him, ratifying it with a ceremony centered on animal sacrifice.

The butchering of animals in the Old Testament seems bizarre to our modern minds, but almost all the disparate groups of ancient peoples offered sacrifices of living things to God or to their gods. The idea is relatively simple, though it was expressed in a wide variety of ceremonies and practices. Some part of the earth is returned to the divine principle — offered up — in order to establish communion with the sacred power. In the Hebrew context, both grain and animals were sacrificed to God.

According to the scholars of Hebrew religious practice, the destruction of grain or animal was meant to signal the sacrificer's offering and rending of himself. The offerer says, in effect, that what is happening to this animal should happen to me if I fall out of friendship with God; or as this animal's life blood is poured out, so I symbolically pour out my own life in devotion and thanksgiving. It is this inner sacrifice that is expressed symbolically through the exterior offering of grain or animal.

The next great covenant that God makes with Israel is associated with Moses and the Exodus from Egypt. God sent Moses to Egypt where his people were enslaved and gave him the charge of leading the captives to freedom. He was to go into the land of oppression, and through his own blood, sweat, and obedience, lead the Israelites back to liberty and right worship. Once they had escaped from oppression, the people, under Moses' leadership, came to Sinai, the mountain of the Lord, where they were given the two tablets of the law. The ten commandments provided instruction for a moral renewal of the tribe. Often the Israelites reacted rather violently against these commands, seeing them as arbitrary external impositions, but God intended them as a sort of sacrifice, a painful but ultimately beneficial remaking of the sinful self. To ratify the people's commitment to the interior sacrifice of the law, Moses ordered an exterior sacrifice of oxen, and splashed the blood from the sacrifice on the altar and on the people. Blood splashed on the people signaled God's pledge of fidelity (his life blood) and splashed on the altar, represented Israel's reciprocal pledge of fidelity to God. Once more the linking of covenant and sacrifice was on display.

The final, great Old Testament covenant with Israel was made with King David after he had proven his faithfulness. The Lord spoke to the king through the prophet Nathan: "I will raise up your offspring after you ... and I will establish his kingdom. Your house and your kingdom shall be made sure forever before me; your throne shall be established forever." (2 Sam. 7:12, 16) This final covenant was accompanied by temple sacrifices for nearly 1,000 years after the death of King David. His immediate successor, Solomon, undertook the enormous project of building a temple to Yahweh in the holy city of Jerusalem. In that place and in the second temple that replaced it, Israelite priests would carry on their sacrificial practice until 70 AD, when the Romans destroyed that second temple.

© 2018 Word on Fire Catholic Ministries

Though covenant and sacrifice were defining elements of ancient Israelite religion and the Jewish people understood themselves in and through these central themes, there was a nagging sense that the covenant had never been truly fulfilled and their sacrifices never completely efficacious. No matter how many times the covenant was taught, renewed, or reaffirmed, it was broken by stubborn Israel, "a stiff-necked people." No matter how many sacrifices were offered in the temple, Yahweh was still not properly honored and the people still not interiorly reformed.

To Abraham, God had promised descendants more numerous that the stars in the sky, and to David, he promised a line of kingly successors, enduring, mysteriously, eternally. Both covenant promises were expressions of the great biblical principle that self-donation leads to the increase of being. These promises would be brought to fulfillment, in the Christian reading, through Christ and his body the Church.

In the New Testament, Jesus is the one who plays the role of the sacrificial lambs offered in the temple and becomes the "once and for all sacrifice" (Heb. 9:26). In accord with the formula of "no communion without sacrifice," Jesus, the covenant in person, is also the sacrificial victim that seals the New Covenant. Pope Leo the Great, writing in the sixth century, gave expression to a patristic commonplace when he said, "There was no other reason for the Son of God becoming flesh than that he should be fixed to the cross." Jesus came, in short, to be the suffering servant who would, through his sacrifice, take away the sins of the world.

Christ makes himself the acceptable sacrifice by pouring out his life so that others may be restored to right relationship to God. Christ's sacrifice fulfilled and completed all of Israel's continual temple sacrifices. Christ's death on the cross is the one, true, and definitive sacrifice that Israel's prophets dreamed would eventually be offered. He is the "Lamb of God, who takes away the sin of the world" (John 1:29).

The Mass, the Eucharistic liturgy, can be understood as an extension or re-presentation of the sacrifice of Jesus, bringing the power of the cross to bear in the present. Those who are gathered around the altar of Christ are not simply recalling Calvary; Calvary has become present to them in all of its spiritual power. Due to the eternity of Christ, there is indeed a kind of collapsing of the dimension of time at the Mass, present meeting past, and both present and past anticipating the future. St. Paul caught this trans-temporality of the Eucharistic liturgy beautifully when, in his First Letter to the Corinthians, he said, "Whenever we eat this bread and drink this cup, we proclaim the death of the Lord until he comes" (1 Cor. 11:26). In other words, here and now, at the Eucharistic assembly, Christ makes present both the past and the future. Indeed, the whole sacrificial history of Israel — from Noah and Abraham through David and Isaiah and Jesus himself — is gathered, summed up, and represented at the Mass.

Christ includes his disciples, despite their weaknesses, in the Eucharist so that they may participate in his perfect sacrifice to the Father [1]. The Eucharist is the sacrifice of right worship through which we share in the Divine Life. By transforming us, it will transform the world.

[1] Joseph Cardinal Ratzinger. *God is Near Us*, (2001, Ignatius, San Francisco), p. 27-34

QUESTIONS FOR UNDERSTANDING

1. What is "covenant" in the Biblical understanding (CCC 356-358)? How did Adam and Eve's relationship with God before the Fall reflect the first covenant?

© 2018 Word on Fire Catholic Ministries

2. Read Genesis 15 and 22. Describe the covenant God made with Abraham. How was the covenant sealed? What are the sacrifices God asked Abraham to undertake as part of the covenant?

3. Why was Israel's sacrifice incomplete? Why was a new covenant necessary? (CCC 578 and 580 and Jer. 31: 31-33)

4. Why is Christ's self-sacrifice perfect, and how is it the fulfillment of Israel's continual temple sacrifices (CCC 613-14 and Isa. 53)?

5. Why was Christ's death on a cross the "once and for all sacrifice" and not merely an execution (Heb. 9: 11-28 and CCC 601-602)? Why is Christ the only one who could effectively make this sacrifice to restore communion with God for all (CCC 616)?

© 2018 Word on Fire Catholic Ministries

6. How is the Eucharist a sacrifice (CCC 1365)? Is the sacrifice of the Mass repeating Christ's sacrifice on the cross again and again (CCC 1366 and 1367)? Explain.

7. How does the Church participate in Christ's sacrifice in the Eucharist (CCC 1368)?

QUESTIONS FOR APPLICATION

1. Reflect on how your daily sacrifices might become united with the perfect and eternal sacrifice of the Mass — the Eucharist. How could this unity help you and others in the Body of Christ?

2. In light of the communion with God that the Eucharist makes possible, why is the liturgy at the heart of social justice? (CCC 1397)

© 2018 Word on Fire Catholic Ministries

REAL PRESENCE
PART I

The *Logos* (Word of God) is manifested within all creation to differing degrees: the beauty of a sunset, the truth of a mathematical equation, the goodness of virtuous living. [1] Through the *Logos*, God reveals himself. The incarnate *Logos*, Christ, is the fullest revelation of God that we can encounter on earth. Christ, the Divine *Logos*, instituted all the Sacraments as the privileged bearers of his presence. This very presence is communicated via the Sacraments in accord with differing degrees of participation, but its fullness is manifested in the Eucharist.

The Eucharist is not simply symbolic of Christ's body and blood; it is his real Body, Blood, Soul, and Divinity in their entirety. Robert Sokolowski beautifully sums up this doctrine: "The Eucharist is the sacramental extension of the Incarnation."[2] As the Fathers at Vatican II pointed out, Christ is indeed present in a variety of ways — in the very intelligibility of the universe, in the gathered assembly at Mass, in the reading of the Scriptures, in the person of the priest — but he is "really, truly, and substantially" present, that is to say, present in a qualitatively different way, in the Eucharistic elements.

Sacraments, according to St. Thomas Aquinas (1225-1274), are types of signs, since they point to something that lies beyond them, namely, the sacred power that flows from the passion of Christ. They are composed of a material element — oil, water, bread, wine, etc. — and a formal element, embodied in the words that accompany them. Thus, baptism is a sacred sign involving the pouring of water and the uttering of the words, "I baptize you in the name of the Father, and of the Son, and of the Holy Spirit," the words specifying the sacred power of Christ operative in and through the water.

Sacraments are not only signs of grace, but actually the instrumental causes of grace. The saving energy of Christ's cross flows, as it were, through these sacred signs, much in the way that the power of the builder flows through the saw that he employs or the authority of the general is made manifest in the soldiers whom he commands. Their function is not merely to display Christ's divine life in a

[1] Joseph Cardinal Ratzinger. *Introduction to Christianity*, (1968, Ignatius, San Francisco), p. 151-52.
[2] Robert Sokolowski. *Christian Faith and Human Understanding*, (2006, CUA, Washington D.C.), p. 72.

form that can be sensed or felt, but they are themselves, through the power of the Holy Spirit, conduits of God's grace flowing from the pierced side of Christ. [3]

Whereas the other sacraments contain only the power of Christ, the Eucharist uniquely contains Christ himself, in the full reality of his presence. As the embodiment of Christ himself, who took on a human nature and surrendered his life as a sacrifice for the redemption of humanity, Vatican II called the Eucharist the "source and summit of the Christian life" (LG 11).

Nevertheless, since the Eucharist is difficult to understand, many disputes about it have arisen throughout the Church's history. The writings of many of the Church Fathers support belief in the Real Presence in the Eucharist. Ignatius of Antioch, Irenaeus, Origin, Ambrose, Augustine and others agree that the word of Christ is the necessary condition for changing the bread and wine into Christ's Body and Blood. However, as time progressed, more technical questions arose as to *how* the Eucharistic change occurs. Berengarius of Tours (999-1088) challenged belief in the Real Presence. Berengarius claimed that there is an essential difference between the historical body of Jesus, born of the Virgin and now reigning in heaven, and the "body" that appears sacramentally on the altar. He thought Christ's presence within the bread and wine was not physical, but that a virtue or spiritual power was added to the elements at the consecration. (Martin Luther argued the same viewpoint many centuries later.) The theory of Berengarius was met almost immediately with strenuous opposition, leading to a synod in 1059 where the theology of Berengarius was condemned based on John 6 and the writings of the Church Fathers.

Even when Jesus first introduced the idea of eating his Body and drinking his Blood to receive eternal life, many disciples could not accept this idea literally due to the abhorrent nature of his statements. Throughout the Old Testament, we can find numerous explicit prohibitions against the eating of flesh and blood. For example, the Mosaic law itself in the books of Leviticus and Deuteronomy states: "It shall be a perpetual statue through your generations, in all of your settlements: you must not eat any fat or any blood" (Lev. 3:17), and "Only be sure that you do not eat the blood; for the blood is the life, and you shall not eat the life with the meat" (Deut. 12:23).

[3] Joseph Cardinal Ratzinger. *God is Near Us*, (2003, Ignatius, San Francisco), p. 43.

© 2018 Word on Fire Catholic Ministries

The Israelites linked the blood with the "life" that came from God and belonged to God, so it was off limits to man. So it's no wonder that many could not accept this teaching.

When some in the crowd quarreled and questioned Jesus' words (John 6:52), he did not soften his speech or describe it as metaphorical. Rather, Jesus clearly says, "Very truly, I tell you, unless you eat the flesh of the Son of Man and drink his blood, you have no life in you" (John 6:53). In that statement, he maintains the potency of his rhetoric by doubling down and using an even stronger Greek word for "eat," which translates as "gnaw" in English. After many desert him, he asks his closest disciples if they will also leave (John 6:67). Although Christ's teaching is difficult and hard to accept, Peter's faith in the Lordship of Jesus (John 6:68) also grounds his faith in *all* that Jesus says.

Jesus also said: "Those who eat my flesh and drink my blood abide in me and I in them. Just as the living Father sent me, and I have life because of the Father, so whoever eats me will live because of me" (John 6:56-57). For Christians, Jesus is not simply a wise teacher by whose words one abides; rather, Jesus is a power in whom we participate, a field of force in which we live and move and have our being. In his master metaphor, St. Paul speaks of the body of Jesus of which baptized people are members (1 Cor 12:12-31). The rhetoric just cited implies an intensely organic relationship between the Father, Jesus, and the Church, the third deriving its life from the second who derives his life from the first. We must eat the flesh and drink the blood of the Lord because that is the way that we come to participate in him and thus, finally in the life of the Father. Elsewhere in John's Gospel, we find equally vitalistic language: we are much more than followers of Jesus; we are grafted onto him as branches are grafted onto a vine (John 15:1-11).

Christ knows the deepest desire of the human heart: the possession of the fullness of the divine life (John 6:26-27). But Christ does not just know this — he is himself the fulfillment of our deepest desire (John 6:49-51). His charity compels him to offer himself as the flesh upon which we feast, so that we may possess the fullness of life (John 6:53). And in literally eating his sacramental Body and Blood, we participate in the fullness of his life. Therefore, we are sanctified and readied for eternal life in the Father through our communion with Christ's divine life in the Eucharist.

QUESTIONS FOR UNDERSTANDING

1. In what varied ways is Christ present in the world and within the Church? What differentiates Christ's presence in the Eucharist from his presence in these other ways (CCC 1373-1374)?

2. What is a Sacrament (CCC 1116 and 1131)? Who instituted the Sacraments?

3. What are the results of receiving the Sacraments, and why are the Sacraments important (CCC 1127-1129)?

© 2018 Word on Fire Catholic Ministries

4. Read the "Bread of Life" discourse in John 6:28-66, and explain in your own words why the Church does not interpret the Eucharist as just a symbol. Pretend you are explaining this to someone who is not Catholic.

5. Why were the Eucharist and the Passion both difficult for the Apostles to accept? What are "stumbling blocks" to accepting them today? (CCC 1336, Isa. 55:8)

QUESTIONS FOR APPLICATION

1. What are some examples of the beauty and intelligibility of God in creation? What does this say about creation's relationship to God and vice versa? How does the possibility of the Incarnation follow from this?

2. Just as we spend our lives seeking truth, beauty, and goodness, how might receiving the Eucharist be the fulfillment of all these desires?

© 2018 Word on Fire Catholic Ministries

3. What value does the Eucharist have in your own life? How do you approach the altar at Mass to receive it? In what ways can you start to cherish the gift of the Eucharist more fully?

NOTES:

© 2018 Word on Fire Catholic Ministries

REAL PRESENCE
PART II

The Church professes in faith that the presence of Christ in the Eucharist is a real presence. This means that "the body and blood together with the soul and divinity of our Lord Jesus Christ, and consequently the whole Christ, is truly, really and substantially contained in the Sacrament of the Most Holy Eucharist."[1]

The presence of Christ is real, but it is not empirically verifiable. This mysterious concept can be better understood with a little insight borrowed from Aristotle's natural philosophy, which St. Thomas Aquinas used in his writings. Aristotle argued that the most basic metaphysical reality is primary substance, an intelligible substrate that lies "underneath" the various accidents or outward appearances of color, shape, size, position, and so forth. So while the secondary qualities of the bread and wine — color, shape, size, aroma — remain unchanged, their underlying, and essentially invisible, substances are transformed into the Body and Blood of Christ.

Why can we believe this? Because Christ said so (John 6:49-57). If Christ is Lord, then what he says *is*. In the biblical reading, God's word does not so much describe as it *achieves*. Thomas Aquinas gave a more philosophical expression to this notion when he said that God does not know things because they exist (as we do) but rather that things exist because God knows them. In the book of Genesis, we hear that creation occurred through a series of divine speech-acts: "God said, 'Let there be light,' and there was light ... God said, 'Let the water under the sky be gathered into a single basin, so that the dry land may appear.' And so it happened ... Then God said, 'Let the earth bring forth all kinds of living creatures ...' And so it happened." (Gen. 1:3, 9, 24). God is not describing a preexisting state of affairs; he is, through his speech, bringing things into being.

Now that very word by which God creates the cosmos became incarnate in Jesus of Nazareth: "And the Word became flesh and made his dwelling among us" (John 1:14). This means that Jesus is not simply a holy man whose words describe God; he is himself the divine Word which affects what it says. Jesus calmed the raging storm with his words; he raised Lazarus from the dead by speaking, "Lazarus, come out!"

[1] Council of Trent (1562), Session 13, can. 1

Again and again, the Gospel writers show us how Jesus' words are efficacious and transformative, producing what they pronounce. Again and again, they present Jesus himself as the incarnation of the creative word of Genesis.

The night before he died, Jesus performed his most extraordinary word-act. Gathered with the twelve for a Passover supper, he "took bread, said the blessing, broke it, and giving it to his disciples, he said, 'Take and eat; this is my body.' Then he took a cup, gave thanks, and gave it to them saying, 'Drink from it, all of you, for this is my blood of the covenant, which will be shed on behalf of many for the forgiveness of sins' " (Matt. 26:26-28). If he were an ordinary prophet or teacher, these powerful words, spoken the night before his death, would have burned themselves into the consciousness of his followers and carried enormous symbolic resonance. But Jesus was not one prophet among many; he was the incarnate Word of God. Therefore, his words had the power to create, to affect reality at the deepest possible level. Since what he says is, the words, "this is my body" and "this is my blood" effectively change the bread and wine into his Body and Blood. Like all divine utterances, they produce what they say.

With the eyes of faith, we can see how the priest, acting in the Person of Christ, speaks Christ's very words at the consecration, and these words make Christ's presence real in the Eucharist. The priest repeats the words of Christ, and by divine power, the bread and wine, at the deepest level of their reality, are changed into the Body and Blood of Christ.

In 1208, Pope Innocent III used the term "transubstantiation" for the first time in an official document, when discussing the use of water and wine at the Eucharist. He remarked that some hold the water to be "transubstantiated into blood" in the process of consecration. Seven years later at the Fourth Lateran Council, the term is employed again: "Jesus Christ, whose body and blood in the sacrament of the altar are truly contained under the appearances of bread and wine, the bread having been transubstantiated into the body and the wine into blood by the divine power" (Fourth Lateran Council [1215], Canon 1).

© 2018 Word on Fire Catholic Ministries

St. Thomas Aquinas addressed the intellectual challenge of faith in the Real Presence of Christ in the Eucharist.[2] Following Aquinas, Bishop Barron explains that the Real Presence of Christ in the Eucharist can be understood in reference to a "participation metaphysic." A "participation metaphysic" is an understanding of reality in which the natural and the supernatural, the finite and the eternal, God and creation, exist in relationship with one another. A distinctly Christian view of this dynamism insists that the relationship is meant to be one of communion and love. The Sacrament of the Eucharist anticipates the transformation at the end times where Christ will be "all in all" (Eph. 1:22-23), while still maintaining the integrity of each creature apart from the Creator.

This most privileged sacrament is necessary for the fullest possible participation in the divine life. Inasmuch as we participate in the Eucharist, we participate in Christ's death and Resurrection. This communion with Christ enables us to share communion with one another, which is the foundation and condition for the unity of the Church as the Body of Christ. The Real Presence unites the Church and thereby makes us signs of Christ in the world.

[2] St. Thomas Aquinas. Summa Theologica, III. q. 75.

QUESTIONS FOR UNDERSTANDING

1. What makes the Eucharist unique and above the other Sacraments (CCC 1324, 1326, 1374)?

2. What is transubstantiation (CCC 1376 and 1412-13)? What is required to accept the doctrine of transubstantiation (CCC 1381)?

3. Why is the Word of Christ, spoken by the priest at the consecration, enough to ensure the transformation of the bread and wine into the Body and Blood of Christ (CCC 1375)?

© 2018 Word on Fire Catholic Ministries

4. How does receiving and communing with Christ through his Body and Blood support the unity of his Mystical Body, the Church (CCC 787-789, 1396)?

5. What is anticipated when we celebrate the Eucharist (CCC 1402-1405)?

QUESTIONS FOR APPLICATION

1. Describe a time in your life when you discovered the difference between *substance* and *accident* or in more contemporary terms, *reality* and *appearance*, when things were "not what they seemed."

2. What does faith in Christ's Real Presence in the Eucharist say about the Catholic view of reality? What is the relationship of the spiritual to the material?

© 2018 Word on Fire Catholic Ministries

3. Why does it make sense that most saints' lives revolved around the Eucharist? Why is the Eucharist necessary for growth in holiness?

4. What positive steps can you take to make the Eucharist the "source and summit" of your own life?

NOTES:

42

© 2018 Word on Fire Catholic Ministries

PRAYERS AFTER
RECEPTION OF THE EUCHARIST

The spiritual transformation that occurs upon reception of the Eucharist at the Holy Sacrifice of the Mass can be more fully realized and appreciated when approached with an attitude of humble and reverent prayer, asking God for the grace to internalize the beautiful, life-giving gift of his Son. Here are some suggestions of traditional prayers to assist you on your spiritual journey.

ANIMA CHRISTI
Attributed to St. Thomas Aquinas

Soul of Christ, sanctify me
Body of Christ, save me
Blood of Christ, inebriate me
Water from Christ's side, wash me
Passion of Christ, strengthen me
O good Jesus, hear me
Within Thy wounds hide me
Suffer me not to be separated from Thee
From the malicious enemy defend me
In the hour of my death call me
And bid me come unto Thee
That I may praise Thee with Thy saints
and with Thy angels
Forever and ever
Amen.

✠ O most loving Jesus, let nothing ever separate me from thee; let me be thine in life and in death; let me be thine forever. *Amen.*

✛ What has passed our lips as food, O Lord, may we possess in purity of heart, that what is given to us in time, be our healing for eternity. May your Body, O Lord, which I have eaten, and your Blood which I have drunk, cleave to my very soul, and grant that no trace of sin be found in me, whom these pure and holy mysteries have renewed. We humbly beseech you, Almighty God, to grant that those whom you refresh with your Sacraments, may serve you worthily by a life well pleasing to you. Through our Lord Jesus Christ, your Son, who lives and reigns, world without end. *Amen.*

✛ I thank you with all my heart, O loving Jesus, for having come to me and allowed me to assist at the Holy Sacrifice of the Mass and to offer it in union with you by receiving your Sacred Body and Most Precious Blood. Grant that I may not forget these graces; let me remember during this day that I have stood beneath your cross, witnessed the renewal of your sacrifice and partaken of the heavenly banquet. May I spend this day for you alone, my Jesus, and perform all my work in union with you according to your words: "He who abides in me, and I in him, he bears much fruit." *Amen.*

✛ Jesus, you are with me only a few moments, but you will have me live with you so intensely during this time, that the character of my life during the rest of the day may be as yours. Please remain in the very center of my soul, not in your bodily presence, but united to my spirit so as to be the source and fountain of all I do. Let me be so united to you that I may think nothing, desire nothing, save what you would have me think and desire. *Amen.*

✛ In your mercy forgive me, O Jesus, and let me not return to the sins I have been committing; help me to guard against my habitual sin and to overcome my ruling passion. Your Precious Blood paid the price of my sins, and gave me the means of all the virtue you wish me to practice in my life. Your Precious Blood is the very life of my soul. Grant that I may use the power of your Precious Blood to bring the living virtues of your heart into mine; let nothing less satisfy me. Make me constant in faith, hope and charity; make my spirit humble and obedient, that I may show forth in my life whose disciple I am; make me patient in adversity that I may bear my cross with resignation to your holy will. *Amen.*

© 2018 Word on Fire Catholic Ministries

BIOGRAPHICAL INFORMATION

BISHOP ROBERT BARRON

Bishop Robert Barron is the founder of Word on Fire Catholic Ministries and the host of CATHOLICISM, a groundbreaking, award-winning documentary about the Catholic Faith. In July 2015, Pope Francis appointed him auxiliary bishop of the Archdiocese of Los Angeles. He previously served as the Rector-President of Mundelein Seminary/University of St. Mary of the Lake from 2012 until 2015.

Bishop Barron's website, WordOnFire.org, reaches millions of people each year. The site hosts daily blog posts, weekly articles and video commentaries, and an extensive audio archive of homilies. Bishop Barron's homilies are heard by tens of thousands of visitors each week. His regular YouTube videos have been viewed millions of times, and thousands of people receive his daily email reflections during Lent and Advent.

EWTN (The Eternal Word Television Network) and CatholicTV broadcast Bishop Barron's videos and documentaries to a worldwide audience of over 150 million people. His weekly Word on Fire radio program has been broadcast in Chicago (WGN) and throughout the country (Relevant Radio — 950 AM Chicago) to over 30 million listeners.

Bishop Barron is a #1 Amazon bestselling author and has published twelve books and hundreds of essays and articles on theology and the spiritual life. He works with NBC News in New York as an on-air contributor and analyst. He is also a frequent commentator for the *Chicago Tribune*, *FOX News*, *CNN*, *EWTN*, *Our Sunday Visitor*, the *Catholic Herald* in London, and *Catholic News Agency*.

Bishop Barron's pioneering work in evangelizing through the new media led Francis Cardinal George to describe him as "one of the Church's best messengers." He has keynoted many conferences and events all over the world, including the opening keynote talk at the 2015 World Meeting of Families.

ROBERT MIXA & ROZANN LEE

Robert Mixa holds a bachelor's degree in philosophy from St. Louis University and a master's degree in theological studies in biotechnology and ethics from the Pontifical John Paul II Institute in Washington, D.C.

Rozann Lee holds a bachelor's degree in theology from the University of Notre Dame and a master's degree in theological studies from the University of Dallas.

NOTES:

© 2018 Word on Fire Catholic Ministries

NOTES:

NOTES:

© 2018 Word on Fire Catholic Ministries